Praying Mantis as Pets Handbook Made Easy:

Full Guide on How to Effectively Raise Praying Mantis as Pets & Other Purposes; Includes Its Care & Gains; Feeding; Choosing Them; Its Home & So On

By

MARKUS J.MUENCH

Copyright@2020

TABLE OF CONTENTS

CHAPTER ONE

INTRODUCTION

From outrageous cover to sexual barbarianism, these devout looking carnivores are as dazzling as they are fearsome.

Named for their conspicuous front legs
that overlay together in a prostrate signal
proposing a demonstration of
commitment, the asking mantis puts on
a show of being peaceful and profound.
You may consider them quiet things,
moving about gradually, snacking on
orchids ... yet, gracious and how it looks
beguile. Actually, Mantis religiosa is a
snare predator; a meat eater with
combative techniques moves and a desire
for live substance. Research says
mantises figure out how to follow
hummingbird feeders for dinners.

With their long necks, upstanding
stance, particular faces and direct look,
they're firmly charming (or startling).
Yet, more than that, they are interesting

animals that have aced their place in the
normal world.

-Regular name: Praying Mantis

-Logical name: Mantis religiosa

-Diet: Carnivore

-Type: Invertebrates

-Normal life span in the wild: 1 years

-SIZE: 0.5 to 6 inches in length

The praying or supplicating mantis is named for its conspicuous front legs, which are twisted and held together at an edge that proposes the situation of petition.

Chasing transformations by any name, these entrancing creepy crawlies are considerable predators. They have three-sided heads balanced on a long "neck," or extended chest. Mantids can blow some people's minds 180 degrees to check their environmental factors with two huge compound eyes and three other straightforward eyes situated between them.

Normally green or earthy colored and very much covered on the plants among which they live, mantis lie in trap or persistently tail their quarry. They utilize their front legs to catch their prey with reflexes so snappy that they are hard to see with the unaided eye. Their legs are further furnished with spikes for trapping prey and sticking it is set up.

Reproducing and conduct

Moths, crickets, grasshoppers, flies, and different bugs are generally the terrible beneficiaries of undesirable mantid consideration. Be that as it may, the bugs will likewise eat others of their own sort. The most popular case of this is the infamous mating conduct of the grown-up female, who some of the time eats her mate soon after—or in any event, during—mating. However this conduct appears not to hinder guys from generation.

Female imploring mantises regularly execute and eat their accomplices during mating.

Imploring mantises stick their casualties at lightning speed.

Imploring mantises once in a while assault hummingbirds.

Numerous old societies held uncommon convictions about the supplicating mantis.

Asking mantises have swelling eyes and heads that can turn 180 degrees.

The praying or supplicating mantis cleans its forelegs subsequent to eating.

The supplicating mantis eats only live food, generally creepy crawlies.

Barbarianism is basic among supplicating mantises.

A supplicating mantis is innocuous to people, however fatal to grasshoppers. Furthermore, a mantis has its own predators to look out for.

CHAPTER TWO
VITAL ATTRIBUTES OF PRAYING MANTIS YOU SHOULD KNOW

i. They have incredible vision

Given the appearance of those peepers, is anyone shocked that they have sound system vision? They can find in 3-D and their eyes each have a fovea – a concentrated territory that permits them to center and track with keenness. Beside those two enormous compound eyes, they additionally have three extra straightforward eyes situated in the middle.

ii. They are dexterous like felines

To the astonishment of researchers recording them, mantises have been found to hop with extraordinary exactness, distorting their body midair to arrive on a tricky and explicit objective.

ii. They make quick work of their prey

Imploring mantises hold on to trap or
persistently tail their prey; however once
they're prepared to strike, they do as
such with lightning speed, assaulting
with those large front legs so rapidly that
it's difficult to see with the unaided eye.
Also, they have spikes on their legs to
stick and pin the casualties into place.

iv. They are experts of camouflage

Asking mantises are especially talented
with regards to cover. They come as
leaves and sticks and branches, in the
same way as other creepy crawlies, yet
additionally take it somewhat further. A
few mantises shed toward the finish of a
dry season to get dark, helpfully
adjusting themselves to the wildfires that
leave a darkened scene. The bloom

mantises are insane; some fiercely
resplendent, others looking so
persuading that clueless bugs come to
gather nectar from them ... furthermore,
become supper meanwhile.

v. They mainly eat live food

Mantises like their food actually moving,
obviously. This makes them
accommodating in bug control as they
sup on a wide range of bugs, including
crickets and grasshoppers.

vi. They upset the natural way of life

In any case, they don't stop at eating
bugs. As referenced above, they normally
target hummingbirds! Also songbirds,
sunbirds, honeyeaters, flycatchers, vireos

and European robins, notwithstanding frogs and reptiles.

vii. They go zombie

All things considered, in their intuition regarding body parts, that is; the point at which they catch fowls, they go straight for the minds.

viii. They do have predators

Despite the fact that they tail hummingbirds and are mind blowing trackers, they are likewise the pursued. Their predators incorporate frogs, reptiles, and fowls, and bugs.

ix. They do fight with bats

Supplicating mantises are additionally gone after by bats, yet they are no simple casualty. They can distinguish the bats' echolocation sounds and when they are drawn nearer, they jump to the ground, regularly executing spirals and circles on their way; whenever got, they attempt to slice their approach to opportunity by utilization of their enormous spiky front legs.

x. They were thought to have extraordinary forces

Indeed, clearly they have unique forces, however early civic establishments, including Ancient Greece, Ancient Egypt, as well as Assyria thought about them to have otherworldly powers. They are frequently described as a femme fatale

xi. They participate in dangerous sex

Dark widows shouldn't get all fun supplicating mantises fiddle with the femme fatale expressions too. Mother mantises lay a particularly enormous pack of eggs, which implies they need a ton of food. This implies, lamentably for their accomplices, they may truly gnaw off their head and eat up them. What's more, they may even do this over the span of their three-hour mating meeting. A smidgen of coital barbarianism may likewise add to the achievement of the fornication.

CHAPTER THREE

DEPENDABLE INSTRUCTIONS TO CARE FOR A PRAYING MANTIS AS A PET

A supplicating mantis is a fun and moderately straightforward pet to think about. There are really various (more than 2,000 and checking) types of mantids. The term asking mantis may have initially alluded to a particular animal types (Mantis religiosa, the European mantis), however now the expression "asking mantid" and "supplicating mantis" is utilized broadly to allude to any of the huge group of mantids. The "supplicating" descriptor emerged from the way that mantids hold their getting a handle on front legs, as though in petition. A few kinds of mantids are accessible for creepy crawly specialists, for example, the African asking mantis species which are reasonable for fledglings.

Maintaining a Praying Mantis as a Pet

Keeping a Praying Mantis as a pet is anything but difficult to do once you become familiar with a couple of things about them. The principal thing you will need to discover is a home for your little pet. You can keep them in a huge vivarium, yet mantises are entirely content in littler nooks with a tallness of approx. 2.5 occasions their length and around multiple times their length in width. So a 2 inch mantis would do well in a compartment 5 inches tall and 4 creeps over. Whatever you keep them in; they will invest the greater part of their energy hanging stylishly, looking out for their prey to draw near enough for them to get them with their raptors. Your mantis will require air, so you should ensure that it is ventilated, yet you don't need the gaps excessively enormous, or your pets' food may get away.

On the off chance that you choose a bigger nook, you will require bunches of things for your pet mantis to move around on. You can utilize pretty much anything, for example, ivy, sticks, and so on... Let your innovativeness direct you. Ensure that the entireties of the things in your mantis walled in area are made sure about, so they won't fall on and harm your pet.

They consume water from water beads right on plant leaves or perhaps from the nook's side. You will water them once per day by moistening within their fenced in area with a splash bottle. It typically just takes 1 or 2 spurts. At that point you can take care of them by putting a fly, cricket or other bug in the nook with them. They ought to be taken care of consistently, yet they won't generally eat, particularly when drawing near to shedding.

In the event that you notice that your pet mantis isn't eating for several days, at that point the person is probably going to shed soon. It is significant that they are not moved or upset right now, as they could fall and it is quite often lethal. So before you contact their holder for taking care of, or moistening them, generally look inside and mind them. When they shed their old exoskeleton they are exceptionally delicate and handily harmed. A couple of hours after they shed, their new exoskeleton will begin to solidify and once you see them moving around, it is protected to hold them once more. It truly is that simple. I trust you appreciate them as much as I do. In the event that you are pondering where to get an imploring mantis, there are a few choices. You could get a wild one, albeit in some cases they are brisk and difficult to get. You could check your nearby pet store and inquire as to whether they convey them.

CHAPTER FOUR

THE GAINS OF HAVING A PRAYING MANTIS YOU SHOULD KNOW

Supplicating mantis are developing in notoriety as pets, as more pet shops stock them, and more pet proprietors start to find their advantages.

The Gains of Keeping Praying Mantis as Pets

Initially, supplicating mantis is totally entrancing to watch. While they may lie unmoving for quite a long time, this is all aspect of a trick; just this is the means by which mantis chase. In nature, they stow away in blossoms and brambles, trusting that a clueless bug will meander past unprepared. Now the mantis lashes out, getting the prey thing with their spiky front legs. Their supper is then secure.

In the home, taking care of your imploring mantis can be a completely retaining, if fairly nerve-wracking, experience.

For such a forceful tracker, mantis can be peculiarly mild with their proprietors. A further advantage of supplicating mantis as pets along these lines is that they can for the most part be taken care of securely. By and large, an imploring mantis will joyfully stroll from hand to hand. In case, you're pondering right presently they're likewise exceptionally far-fetched to attempt to remove a lump from your finger.

The main stipulation here is that the grown-ups create wings so they are fit for taking off in the event that you bother them. At the end of the day, while you can securely deal with youths, with regards to holding the grown-ups, attempt to guarantee your windows are shut to keep away from escapees.

Finally, continuing supplicating mantis as pets offers you a chance to enter a different universe. Keeping a supplicating mantis can be fairly similar to having your own zoo; you get the chance to watch your pet growing up, chasing, changing its skin, and arriving at development. In case you're fortunate, you'll even have a chance to raise these intriguing bugs and watch the entire hover of life finished. For the individuals who appreciate observing all the action and life in a fish tank, supplicating mantis can be similarly captivating.

Fortunately, with a couple of basic pieces of gear and a little work on, supplicating mantis are likewise very simple to keep as pets. This can make them considerably additionally enticing prisoners...

CHAPTER FIVE

THE DEVICES/EQUIPMENT YOU REQUIRE TO EFFECTIVELY KEEP A PRAYING MANTIS PLUS THE FOOD THEY NEED, AND OTHERS FACTS

Step by step instructions to keep a Praying Mantis as a Pet

To effectively keep a pet supplicating mantis you will require the accompanying bits of gear/devices:

-An enclosure

-A roost

-A houseplant splash

-A radiator

-Some food

With simply this short shopping list you'll be well en route to supplicating mantis achievement.

We should investigate every single one of these components thus, so you know precisely what supplies you'll be requiring for your new pet.

Pens for Praying Mantis

The main bit of hardware that you will to buy is some type of "enclosure" or vivarium in which to keep your pet

mantis. Grown-up mantis can be kept
effectively in little fish tanks made of
glass or plastic. Then again, plastic sweet
containers can make appropriate pens.

More youthful mantis will be littler, and
any unmistakable plastic or glass holder
can make a helpful confine. Indeed, even
clear plastic drinking tumblers – as sold
for grills – can be utilized effectively if
the mouth is secured by a bit of net
window ornament material hung on with
a flexible band.

Whatever you pick as a pen for your
supplicating mantis, you should
guarantee that it adjusts to various
brilliant guidelines.

Right off the bat, the enclosure ought to keep your pet from getting away, however it ought to likewise permit some air development. Stale, wet air can slaughter supplicating mantis so it is fundamental that some sort of ventilation is available. For instance, on account of the plastic sweet container referenced already, it is savvy to puncture the top with a sewing needle or fastening iron so clammy air can get away.

The second significant factor while picking an imploring mantis confine is that it ought to be at any rate twice as tall as your mantis is long. There is a straightforward purpose behind this; when an imploring mantis changes its skin, it stays its back feet to the head of the enclosure, parts its old skin down the back and afterward gradually slides out of the skin. The pen must be twice as tall as your pet is long to permit it to appropriately slide out of the old skin. Without this, mantis can neglect to shed appropriately, a medical issue that can cause demise may come in.

Roosts for Praying Mantis

Supplicating mantis once in a while have a sense of security on the floor; in nature they climb up plants to remain safe. The equivalent is valid in imprisonment; not exclusively will your mantis feel more secure off the ground, yet these roosts are additionally significant for shedding and for chasing.

In enormous grown-up mantis, the most effortless roost is to put a few twigs in the enclosure that your mantis can sit on. In littler confines a reasonable substitute can include balancing a bit of kitchen move down within the compartment. Whatever alternative you pick, the roost ought to permit your mantis to sit up high, yet ought to likewise be open from the base of the confine. Thusly, if your mantis falls, you can be sure that it will have the option to discover its way back up once more.

A Houseplant Spray

Asking mantis is probably not going to drink from a water bowl like a canine or a snake. Rather, they will in general beverage water beads right away from the outside of plants. The simplest method to copy this is imprisonment is using a houseplant splash firearm.

Essentially shower within your mantis confine gently several times each week so as to permit your mantis to drink from the beads. After some time the extra beads will dissipate out, fit to be supplanted with the following showering.

It merits referencing that when an imploring mantis sheds, it needs a higher dampness than ordinary. In the event that you actually notice that your pet mantis has gone off its food, in this manner, consider giving it an additional shower. That will assist with expanding the surrounding mugginess inside the enclosure and make shedding simpler.

A Heater

Supplicating mantises originate from warm atmospheres, so will in general do best with counterfeit warming. This is commonly just required in the winter months; over summer the surrounding temperature in your home ought to be completely adequate for your pet.

Purchasing a radiator for your pet needn't be costly; numerous reptile shops sell low-fueled warmth cushions that cost pennies every day to run, and are completely protected to leave on long haul, yet will keep your pet warm and hot.

Nourishment for Praying Mantis

Pet imploring mantises are carnivores; they need live food to eat in the event that they are to flourish in bondage. This is the one expected drawback of keeping a pet mantis; you'll have to feel great purchasing tubs of creepy crawlies to take care of, and you'll should be sufficiently certain to forfeit live bugs consistently.

You can't over-feed a mantis so fundamentally simply feed it as much as it will eat. This regularly implies including a couple of crickets, container insects or flies to the enclosure consistently. Now you will have the option to watch your mantis chase for its supper.

Note that you shouldn't leave live-food in the pen for the long haul as this may worry your mantis. Any uneaten food ought to be eliminated inside an hour or so to forestall this happening.

As referenced already, after some time your mantis will develop and change its skin. This shedding cycle is quite often gone before by fasting. On the off chance that your mantis actually quits eating, at that point, almost certainly, it is coming up to changing its skin. As of now it is especially significant that no uneaten food is left in the enclosure, as it might make harm to your fragile, newly shed mantis. Happy mantis raising!

THE END

* 9 7 9 8 6 8 7 8 5 2 8 5 2 *